CONTEMPORARY AMERICAN SUCCESS STORIES

Famous People of Hispanic Heritage

Volume V

Barbara J. Marvis

A Mitchell Lane
Multicultural Biography Series
• Celebrating Diversity •

CONTEMPORARY AMERICAN SUCCESS STORIES
Famous People of Hispanic Heritage

<table>
<tr>
<td>

VOLUME I
Geraldo Rivera
Melissa Gonzalez
Federico Peña
Ellen Ochoa
</td>
<td>

VOLUME II
Tommy Nuñez
Margarita Esquiroz
Cesar Chavez
Antonia Novello
</td>
<td>

VOLUME III
Giselle Fernandez
Jon Secada
Desi Arnaz
Joan Baez
</td>
<td>

VOLUME IV
Selena Quintanilla Pérez
Robert Rodriguez
Josefina López
Alfredo Estrada
</td>
<td>

VOLUME V
Gloria Estefan
Fernando Cuza
Rosie Perez
Cheech Marin
</td>
</tr>
<tr>
<td>

VOLUME VI
Pedro José Greer
Nancy Lopez
Rafael Palmeiro
Hilda Perera
</td>
<td>

VOLUME VII
Raul Julia
Mariah Carey
Andres Galarraga
Mary Joe Fernandez
</td>
<td>

VOLUME VIII
Cristina Saralegui
Trent Dimas
Nydia Velázquez
Jimmy Smits
</td>
<td>

VOLUME IX
Roy Benavidez
Isabel Allende
Oscar De La Hoya
Jackie Guerra
</td>
<td>

VOLUME X
Rebecca Lobo
Carlos Mencia
Linda Chavez Thompson
Bill Richardson
</td>
</tr>
</table>

Publisher's Cataloging in Publication
Marvis, Barbara J.
    Famous people of Hispanic heritage. Vol. V / Barbara J. Marvis
    p. cm. —(Contemporary American success stories)—(A Mitchell Lane
multicultural biography series)
    Includes index.
    LCCN: 95-75963
    ISBN: 1-883845-32-7 (hc)
    ISBN: 1-883845-31-9 (pbk)

    1. Hispanic Americans—Biography—Juvenile literature. 1. Title.
II. Series.

E184.S75M37 1996

920'.009268
QBI96-20404

Illustrated by Barbara Tidman
Project Editor: Susan R. Scarfe

Mitchell Lane
PUBLISHERS
Your Path To Quality Educational Material

P.O. Box 200
Childs, Maryland 21916-0200

TABLE OF CONTENTS

Acknowledgments

Every reasonable effort has been made to gain copyright permission where such permission has been deemed necessary. Any oversight brought to the publisher's attention will be corrected in future printings.

Most of the stories in this series were written through personal interviews and/or with the complete permission of the person, representative of the person, or family of the person being profiled and are authorized biographies. Though we attempted to contact personally each and every person profiled within, for various reasons we were unable to authorize every story. All stories have been thoroughly researched and checked for accuracy, and to the best of our knowledge represent true stories.

We wish to acknowledge with gratitude the generous help of Elaine DagenBela and MaryRose Walls of the Hispanic Heritage Awards for their recommendations of those we have profiled in this series. Our greatest appreciation also goes to Lourdes Lopez (Estefan Enterprises) for her help in developing our story of Gloria Estefan; Fernando Cuza (telephone interview April 4, 1996, and others) for help with our story and photographs of Fernando Cuza; and Cheech Marin (telephone interview May 17, 1996) and Andie Shechter for their time and help in profiling Cheech Marin.

Photograph Credits

The quality of the photographs in this book may vary; many of them are personal snapshots supplied to us courtesy of the person being profiled. Many are very old, one-of-a-kind photos. Most are not professional photographs, nor were they intended to be. The publisher felt that the personal nature of the stories in this book would only be enhanced by real-life, family album–type photos, and chose to include many interesting snapshots, even if they were not quite the best quality. p.11 Bettmann; p.17 Raul de Molina, Shooting Star; p.21 AP/Wide World Photos; p.23 courtesy Estefan Enterprises; p.25 AP/Wide World Photos; p.28 Bettmann; p.31 courtesy Estefan Enterprises; p.32 Fitzroy Barrett, Globe Photos; p.33 Raul de Molina, Shooting Star; p.37, p.39, p.40, p.41, p.44, p.45, p.46, p.49, p.50, p.54, p.55, p.56, p.60, p.61, p.62, p.63 courtesy Fernando Cuza; p.71, p.72, p.74, p.75, p.76, p.83, p.84, p.87 the Kobal Collection; p.89 courtesy Cheech Marin; p.91 the Kobal Collection; p.92 courtesy Miramax Films; p.93 courtesy CBS

About the Author

Barbara Marvis has been a professional writer for twenty years. Motivated by her own experience with ethnic discrimination as a young Jewish girl growing up in suburban Philadelphia, Ms. Marvis developed the **Contemporary American Success Stories** series to dispel racial and ethnic prejudice, to tell culturally diverse stories that maintain ethnic and racial distinction, and to provide positive role models for young minorities. She is the author of several books for young adults, including **Tommy Nuñez: NBA Referee/Taking My Best Shot**. She holds a B.S. degree in English and communications from West Chester State University and an M.Ed. in remedial reading from the University of Delaware.

INTRODUCTION

by Kathy Escamilla

One of the fastest growing ethno-linguistic groups in the United States is a group of people who are collectively called Hispanic. The term *Hispanic* is an umbrella term that encompasses people from many nationalities, from all races, and from many social and cultural groups. The label *Hispanic* sometimes obscures the diversity of people who come from different countries and speak different varieties of Spanish. Therefore, it is crucial to know that the term *Hispanic* encompasses persons whose origins are from Spanish-speaking countries, including Spain, Mexico, Central and South America, Cuba, Puerto Rico, the Dominican Republic, and the United States. It is important also to note that Spanish is the heritage language of most Hispanics. However, Hispanics living in the United States are also linguistically diverse. Some speak mostly Spanish and little English, others are bilingual, and some speak only English.

Hispanics are often also collectively called Latinos. In addition to calling themselves Hispanics or Latinos, many people in this group also identify themselves in more specific terms according to their country of origin or their ethnic group (e.g., Cuban-American, Chicano, Puerto Rican–American, etc.). The population of Hispanics in the United States is expected to triple in the next twenty-five years, making it imperative that students in schools understand and appreciate the enormous contributions that persons of Hispanic heritage have made in the Western Hemisphere in general and in the United States in particular.

There are many who believe that in order to be successful in the United States now and in the twenty-first century, all persons from diverse cultural backgrounds, such as Hispanics, should be assimilated. To be assimilated means losing one's distinct cultural and linguistic heritage and changing to or adopting the cultural attributes of the dominant culture.

Others disagree with the assimilationist viewpoint and believe that it is both possible and desirable for persons from diverse cultural backgrounds to maintain their cultural heritage and also to contribute positively and successfully to the dominant culture. This viewpoint is called cultural pluralism, and it is from the perspective of cultural pluralism that these biographies are written. They represent persons who identify strongly with their Hispanic heritage and at the same time who are proud of being citizens of the United States and successful contributors to U.S. society.

The biographies in these books represent the diversity of Hispanic heritage in the United States. Persons featured are contemporary figures whose national origins range from Argentina to Arizona and whose careers and contributions cover many aspects of contemporary life in the United States. These biographies include writers, musicians, actors, journalists, astronauts, businesspeople, judges, political activists, and politicians. Further, they include Hispanic women and men, and thus also characterize the changing role of all women in the United States. Each person profiled in this book is a positive role model, not only for persons of Hispanic heritage, but for any person.

Collectively, these biographies demonstrate the value of cultural pluralism and a view that the future strength of the United States lies in nurturing the diversity of its human potential, not in its uniformity.

Dr. Kathy Escamilla is currently Vice President of the National Association for Bilingual Education and an Associate Professor of Bilingual Education and Multicultural Education at the University of Colorado, Denver. She previously taught at the University of Arizona, and was the Director of Bilingual Education for the Tucson Unified School District in Tucson, Arizona. Dr. Escamilla earned a B.A. degree in Spanish and Literature from the University of Colorado in 1971. Her master's degree is in bilingual education from the University of Kansas, and she earned her doctorate in bilingual education from UCLA in 1987.

MAP OF THE WORLD

PACIFIC OCEAN

AUSTRALIA

ASIA

INDIAN OCEAN

EUROPE

AFRICA

SPAIN

GREENLAND

ATLANTIC OCEAN

DOMINICAN REPUBLIC

PUERTO RICO

SOUTH AMERICA

CANADA

NORTH AMERICA

UNITED STATES

CUBA

MEXICO

PACIFIC OCEAN

HAWAII

7

GLORIA ESTEFAN

Recording Artist, Songwriter

1957-

"I'm an example of a Cuban-American who has grown up in the United States having the best of both worlds because we've been inspired by the business mind and the unbelievable freedom of the Anglo world, but we have a lot of our own ethnic flavor. **"**

Gloria Estefan, 1994

BIO HIGHLIGHTS

- Born September 1, 1957, in Havana, Cuba; mother: Gloria Fajardo; father: José Manuel Fajardo
- Family fled Castro's Cuba in 1959; father had been part of the Batista regime
- Grew up in Miami, Florida
- Father was captured in Cuba in Bay of Pigs incident
- Father fought in Vietnam and returned home ill after having been exposed to Agent Orange
- Joined Emilio Estefan's band, the Miami Latin Boys, in 1975. The band became the Miami Sound Machine (MSM)
- Married Emilio Estefan on September 1, 1978
- MSM released first album *Renacer*
- 1981, signed with Discos CBS International to release Spanish-language albums
- 1982, "Dr. Beat" climbed to number ten on the dance charts
- 1984, released first album in English, *Eyes of Innocence*
- *Primitive Love* (1985) was her first successful U.S. English-language album
- January 1990, performed at the American Music Awards and the Grammy Award ceremonies
- March 1990, MSM earned the Crystal Globe Award
- March 20, 1990, a bus accident in Pennsylvania left Gloria badly injured
- January 1991, returned to performing with her appearance on the American Music Awards
- September 1995, gave concert to U.S. camp in Guantánamo Bay in Cuba
- July 18, 1996, performed at the Olympics
- Currently: married to Emilio Estefan; they have two children: son Nayib was born in 1980; daughter Emily was born in 1994

GLORIA ESTEFAN

"**S**he is Miami's Mother Teresa," says Dr. Mary Louise Cole of the Children's Home Society of Florida when asked about Gloria Estefan. "The children in our care are fortunate that Gloria and Emilio have both given so completely of themselves for their benefit."

Laurie Kaye, Director of Development for the group that helps abused and neglected youngsters, gives Gloria credit for the very existence of Children's Home Society. "Gloria and her husband have done wonders for us," she says. "I wish there were more Gloria Estefans."

Known to most of the world as the queen of Latin pop, singing star Gloria Estefan is also a timeless angel of mercy. People throughout Miami call her "a star with a heart." She devotes herself to helping others—from those devastated by Hurricane Andrew to the battered children of Miami whose cries are unheard because luck or their parents ran out on them.

"I've seen things that have ruined the lives of children," says Gloria. "I've seen kids who are abused by their parents, who run away from home and then go on to abuse their own kids. It's a vicious circle."

Gloria is passionate about her charitable work. In fact, she continued her work with sick and needy children even when she was recovering from the debilitating injuries she suffered in a near-fatal bus accident while she was on tour in 1990. Her back had been broken, but her spirit never was. In 1992, she was named

▼▼▼▼▼▼
Known to most of the world as the queen of Latin pop, Gloria Estefan is also a timeless angel of mercy.
▲▲▲▲▲▲

Humanitarian of the Year by B'nai B'rith. The same year, readers of *Vista,* The Hispanic Magazine voted her Hispanic Woman of the Year. In 1993, she received a well-deserved star on the Hollywood Walk of Fame.

"I'm an example of a Cuban-American who has grown up in the United States," says Gloria, "having the best of both worlds because we've been inspired by the business mind and the unbelievable freedom of the Anglo world, but we have a lot of our own ethnic flavor."

Gloria Maria Fajardo was born on September 1, 1957, in Havana, Cuba. She is the firstborn daughter of Gloria and José Manuel Fajardo. She has a younger sister, Rebecca (Becky). While she was growing up, Gloria was often called Glorita ("Little Gloria") to distinguish her from her mother.

Gloria's mother was a kindergarten teacher in Cuba. Her father was a career military officer under President Fulgencio Batista y Zaldívar. He had even served as a personal escort to Batista's wife during the dictator's regime. But everything changed in January 1959 when Fidel Castro and his soldiers defeated Batista's army and gained control of the government in the name of the Cuban people. Batista

In 1993, Gloria received a star on the Hollywood Walk of Fame. Shown in back from left to right are recording star Celia Cruz; Gloria's mother, Gloria Fajardo; and Gloria's husband, Emilio.

Just a few days after Castro assumed control of the Cuban government, the Fajardos traveled by ferryboat to Texas.

GLORIA ESTEFAN

had always had the support of the United States government, but when Castro seized power, he announced that his new government would align itself with the Soviet Union. Cuba would be governed according to communist principles. This spelled disaster for many middle- and upper-class citizens of Cuba, especially business owners who were forced to give their businesses to the government. It was especially disastrous for members of Batista's regime, who faced imprisonment, or even death, if they remained in Cuba. Many fled the island. Among them were the Fajardos.

Just a few days after Castro assumed control of the Cuban government, the Fajardos traveled by ferryboat to Texas. Gloria was only sixteen months old. "I was a baby," she says. "I don't remember much at all."

The family lived in Texas for only a short time. They moved to South Carolina, and, finally, in 1960, to Miami, when Gloria was two years old. Though Gloria was only a toddler when all of this happened, she does remember her father's politics many years later. "He believed in freedom," she says. "He was a very political man. He believed Castro was wrong. He wanted me to be safe [and brought me to the U.S.], then he wanted to go back and save Cuba."

The Fajardos thought their stay in the United States would be a brief one. They thought of themselves as exiles instead of immigrants, seeking a safe haven until it was okay to return to

Cuba. They were sure Castro would be quickly overthrown. They did not apply for U.S. citizenship, nor did they attempt to blend with U.S. culture. But Gloria's father did try to save Cuba.

In 1961, various leaders of the Batista government who were exiled in the United States got together with representatives of the U.S. government to overthrow Castro. The United States supported the effort because they hoped to replace Castro with someone who was friendly to the United States. On April 17, 1961, 1,300 Cuban exiles sailed secretly from the United States to *Bahia de Cochinos* (Bay of Pigs) on Cuba's southwest shore. José Fajardo was among them. But Castro was expecting them: the mission was no secret to him. When it looked like the mission would fail, the U.S. withdrew its support. The rebels were easily defeated by Castro's army and more than 1,100 exiles were taken prisoner. José Fajardo was among them, too.

Gloria and her mother were alone in the United States. José spent nearly two years in prison in Cuba. Just a few days before Christmas in 1962, he returned to Miami—President John F. Kennedy had made a deal with Castro, exchanging prisoners for medicine and food.

Even when José returned to Miami, life in the United States was difficult for the family. The Fajardos spoke only Spanish, and they were faced with many negative attitudes from U.S. citizens at the time.

José spent nearly two years in prison in Cuba.

At school she quickly learned English and caught up with the other children. She even won an award for her writing skills.

GLORIA ESTEFAN

Gloria was determined to succeed. At school she quickly learned English and caught up with the other children. She even won an award for her writing skills. All through school she excelled. She attended an all-girls Catholic high school in Miami, where she made honor roll every semester. She eventually received a partial scholarship to the University of Miami.

But her home life was especially difficult. When her father returned home from the Bay of Pigs disaster, he enlisted in the U.S. Army, quickly rose to the rank of captain, and in 1966 volunteered for duty in Vietnam. Gloria asked her father why he was going away again. Why did he volunteer for Vietnam?

"With what faith could I ask the United States to help free Cuba, if I am not willing to help the U.S.," her father replied. José served in Vietnam for two years, returning home in 1968, when Gloria was ten.

As soon as he came home, the family noticed there was something wrong with him. Though he had not been injured in combat, he was not acting like himself. "He'd fall for no reason," Gloria remembers. "He was diagnosed with multiple sclerosis, but it may have been related to Agent Orange. There were some things he experienced that simply didn't make sense with MS." When he was in Vietnam, José had been exposed to a chemical defoliant that the U.S. military used to kill the leaves of trees and plants where the enemy would hide. Many soldiers who had come in contact with the chemical later developed cancer and other crippling diseases.

Within a few months, her father was confined to bed and Gloria's mother was forced to seek work to support the family. She worked as a clerk while she returned to college to obtain an American teaching degree. Then she taught public school in Miami. From the time she was eleven until she was sixteen, Gloria took care of her father and her younger sister after school. José Fajardo required constant care.

"It was around the clock," says Gloria. "It wasn't easy. His mind went before his body. There were times when he wasn't aware of who I was, or who any of us were. It was very hard. Then it just gets to the point where you pray that the suffering will end, because you can't imagine why anyone has to go through something like that." For the last five years of his life, her father was in the Veterans Administration Hospital, where he died in 1980.

As a teenager, Gloria would sometimes retreat to her bedroom and listen to music for hours on end. She loved to sing along with the ballads and pop songs. She learned to play the guitar, and soon she was good enough to play along with her favorite songs on her mother's records or on the radio. "When my father was ill, music was my escape," Gloria remembers. "It was my release from everything. I'd lock myself up in my room with my guitar."

▼▼▼▼▼▼
As a teenager, Gloria would sometimes retreat to her bedroom and listen to music for hours on end.
▲▲▲▲▲▲

▼▼▼▼▼

One day, when she was a high-school senior, a popular band leader named Emilio Estefan visited Gloria's high school.

▲▲▲▲▲▲

Gloria had an increasing love of music. One day, when she was a high-school senior, a popular band leader named Emilio Estefan visited Gloria's high school. She remembers being very interested when he spoke. Just a few weeks later, Gloria and several of her friends decided to put a band together themselves to play for a party. The father of one of the other band members knew Emilio, and he invited him to come over to one of their rehearsals. "I met him first when he came to give some pointers to some friends and me about getting a band together for a party. Then, three months later, my mother dragged me to this wedding that I really didn't want to go to, and Emilio's band was playing. They were called the Miami Latin Boys. Emilio remembered me and asked me to sing a song with the band." By now, Gloria was graduated from high school, and she was thinking about college. She was not thinking about joining a band. In fact, at the time, bands rarely featured females at all. But just a few weeks later, in October 1975, Emilio called Gloria and asked her to join his band.

"I went with my grandma, my mom, and my sister to this tiny apartment where Emilio lived with his parents," Gloria recalls. "The band was in the living room and the neighbors were dancing outside." Gloria sang for the band, and they all decided they liked her.

Emilio Estefan had come to America with his family in 1967. They had left Cuba in 1965 and spent two years in Spain trying to gain legal entry to the United States. When Emilio was fifteen, his family moved to Miami. Like many other Cuban refugees, the family was very poor when they arrived. Emilio took a number of jobs to help support the family. Eventually, he found steady employment at Bacardi Imports, where he was hired as a clerk. He worked his way up the corporate ladder to become the company's director of marketing. But he had always had a different dream. His real passion was music. Before he left Cuba, he had had a band with some friends. While he was working at Bacardi, he formed another band. The band played at parties and dance clubs. By 1974, Emilio's band was one of the most popular dance bands in Miami. Emilio began to think about quitting his job with Bacardi and devoting all his time to making music. Eventually, that's just what he did.

Gloria and Emilio were married in 1978.

When Emilio first asked Gloria to join his band as the vocalist, she said no. She was just a freshman at the University of Miami, and she was worried that she would not have sufficient time for her studies—so was her mother. But Emilio assured Gloria that she would only perform on weekends and vacations. Her mother consented only if Gloria agreed to finish her degree, which she did. "I loved music so much that I couldn't

"All of a sudden, I was going to parties every weekend, singing with the whole band behind me," remembers Gloria.

let a great opportunity like this pass me by," she says.

When Gloria became the band's lead vocalist, she gave the group a very distinctive sound. Within weeks, Emilio changed the band's name to the Miami Sound Machine. "All of a sudden, I was going to parties every weekend, singing with the whole band behind me," remembers Gloria. She enjoyed herself immensely. She had never given much thought to a career in music. Gloria had majored in psychology in college because she thought she wanted to be a psychologist. Though she did get her degree, she later learned that music was her lifelong avocation.

Through their music, Emilio and Gloria got to know each other. "I was attracted to him right away," remembers Gloria, "but I didn't dwell on it because I thought it would never happen. He was my boss in the band for almost a year and a half before we started dating." That was in July 1976. They dated for another two years. In May 1978, Gloria graduated from college. On September 1, 1978, she and Emilio were married.

Later that year, Emilio and Gloria traveled back to Cuba to help Emilio's brother and his family leave the country. It was the first time she had been back since she was a baby. "For me there was an overwhelming claustrophobic feeling there; it made me very sad," she says.

The Miami Sound Machine released their first album in 1978 for a local label. *Renacer* was a collection of disco, pop, and original ballads sung in Spanish. At this time, the band consisted of Marcos Avila on bass, Kiki Garcia on drums, Raul Murciano on keyboard and saxophone, Emilio on keyboard, and Gloria as vocalist. The band became popular among local fans. Over the next two years, the band released two more albums, each one selling well locally, but none gaining much attention elsewhere.

Many things happened for Gloria in 1980; some were sad events and some were happy. After twelve years of crippling illness, José Fajardo died from complications relating to multiple sclerosis. His long illness had brought much grief to the family.

But there was much happiness in 1980 as well. After two years of marriage, Gloria and Emilio had a son. They named him Nayib. Both of them immediately felt their son was the most important responsibility in their lives. Shortly after their son's birth, Emilio quit his secure job at Bacardi Imports to devote himself full-time to the Miami Sound Machine. He knew the band required his full attention if it were ever to become a success. Soon the group signed a contract with Discos CBS International, the Miami-based Hispanic division of CBS Records.

Discos CBS International specializes in Latin music. Company officials decided that the Miami Sound Machine should only release albums in Spanish. They planned to distribute the band's recordings in the mostly Spanish-speaking countries of Latin America. Between 1981 and 1984,

▼▼▼▼▼▼
The Miami Sound Machine released their first album in 1978 for a local label.
▲▲▲▲▲▲

Between 1981 and 1984, the group recorded four Spanish-language albums that spurred a dozen hit songs around the world.

the group recorded four Spanish-language albums that spurred a dozen hit songs around the world. At first, the band members were disappointed that they could not gain the wider listening audience in the U.S. Gloria explains: "CBS thought we would sell better in Latin America if we sang in Spanish. But we kept the right to record in English, because eventually we wanted to try again for the States. But first we decided to concentrate on the Latin-American end because it was becoming very successful." Soon they were one of the most popular bands in Latin America.

By 1982, Emilio had stopped performing with the band. He wanted to focus on breaking the group out of the Latin market, and he wanted to care for their son while Gloria was performing. The band was convinced they could attract a following in the United States if they were only given a chance. In 1984, their songwriter, Kiki Garcia, wrote a song called "Dr. Beat." It was a Latin-style dance song that the group planned to release as a single. But Kiki wrote the song in English and translated it into Spanish. The Spanish words would not fit the melody, so the group persuaded CBS to let them release the song in English. CBS said okay, but they would only release it as the B side of a Spanish ballad. Usually, the B side gets no air time on radio, but "Dr. Beat" was soon heard on radio stations all over Miami. Many Spanish-language stations played the English-language song, and soon several English-language channels aired it as well. CBS was encouraged by the response, and they released "Dr. Beat" on a 12-inch dance single. The song went all the way to number ten on the dance charts.

CBS finally agreed to let the group release an entire album in English. In 1984, the Miami Sound Machine recorded *Eyes of Innocence.* It was not until August 1985, however, when the band released *Primitive Love,* that the group first enjoyed international recognition and success in the United States. One of the songs on that album, "Conga," was released as a single and went to number ten on the American pop charts. Even more surprising to the group, the song appeared on

Gloria is an enthusiastic performer.

Billboard's dance, Latin, and Black charts as well, making it the first song in history to appear on four charts at the same time. It became their

"It looked like an overnight success because of 'Conga,'" recalls Gloria, "but we had been working for years."

breakout hit. The Miami Sound Machine seemed to be an overnight success.

"It looked like an overnight success because of 'Conga,'" recalls Gloria, "but we had been working for years. 'Conga' was on our tenth album." Shortly after, "Bad Boy" was released as a single, and it too enjoyed success, soaring to number ten on the pop charts.

Gloria was not entirely happy with her new success, however. "You can't build a career on congas," she later explained, "even in the Hispanic market. It's one thing once a night, at the end . . . and that's it—you don't do ten." What Gloria really wanted to do was perform the ballads and love songs she had loved as a kid. Finally, she got her chance when "Words Get in the Way" was released as the third single from *Primitive Love*. This song became a hit as well.

In 1987, the group released the album *Let It Loose*, which sold three million copies in the United States and produced four top-ten hits. It stayed on the pop charts for more than two years, and the band spent 20 months touring the United States and the rest of the world to promote it. At the end of the tour, they returned to Miami to perform two local concerts to sold-out audiences. But for the first time, Emilio did not accompany Gloria and the band on the tour. He decided he should remain at home to increase his role as a producer. In addition, the couple had always taken Nayib out of school to tour, and they decided that if Emilio stayed home, Nayib could remain in school.

It was lonely for Gloria to be traveling without her family. She spent many of her nights on the road writing songs. Over the years, Gloria had received increasing recognition for her songwriting talents, and several of her songs had been released on previous albums. *Cuts Both Ways,* released in 1989, contained ten songs written by Gloria. The album was a smash hit. But her experience touring without Emilio and Nayib led to her decision that subsequent tours would include her family. She did not like touring without them.

The Miami Sound Machine originally released songs in Spanish for the Latin-American market.

Because of her family's experiences with the Cuban government, Gloria grew to dislike political causes. "I hate politics," she says. "It can never be completely honest. I've lost too much to politics already—my father, my family's peace of mind." But in 1988, Gloria found herself in the middle of a political uprising caused by the Cuban government when the Cuban coaches protested Miami Sound Machine's performance at the closing of the Pan American Games. They wanted a Latin-American band. "I wasn't going to back down," Gloria says. "That would have been silly. We were a perfectly logical choice to play. We were known all over Latin America."

GLORIA ESTEFAN

Gloria
performed
at the
American
Music
Awards and
the Grammy
Award
ceremonies
in January
of 1990.

The group went on to play at the conclusion of the games, and they received overwhelming support. "I don't like to get my music involved with politics," Gloria explains. "Of course, I can't divorce myself from my heritage. I realize that brings with it certain political tensions. But you can't destroy yourself with hatred. I weigh things out and I try to make the best decisions for me and my family." One of those decisions is that she will never perform in Cuba. She feels she would be betraying her father if she did.

Gloria performed at the American Music Awards and the Grammy Award ceremonies in January of 1990. In March, the Miami Sound Machine was awarded the Crystal Globe by CBS, which is given to performers who sell more than five million records outside their own country. On March 19, Gloria was a guest at the White House, where she was honored by President George Bush for her drug prevention work with teenagers. Things had never looked brighter for Gloria and Emilio. But on the following day, tragedy struck.

On March 20, 1990, the Miami Sound Machine were on their way to Syracuse, New York, where they were scheduled to perform a concert. Gloria did not like to fly, and the group always traveled by bus. She felt safer that way. "If you crash, at least you're not falling thirty-seven thousand feet," she said.

It was snowing as the bus traveled I-380 through the Pocono Mountains near Tobyhanna, a small town in eastern Pennsylvania not far from the New York State line. On the bus that day were Gloria, Emilio, Nayib, who was nine at the time, Nayib's tutor, and Gloria's assistant, Jelissa Arencibia. The tour bus stopped because there was an accident ahead blocking the road. A tractor trailer had jackknifed across the road, and the bus stopped to wait for the accident to be cleared. The tour bus was hit from behind. Gloria was thrown from the couch where she had been lying down. Emilio had been talking on his cellular phone. There was a second crash as the tour bus was pushed into the truck parked ahead of it on the road. The front of the bus caved in.

On March 19, 1990, Gloria was a guest at the White House and was honored by President George Bush. Her son, Nayib, and husband, Emilio, accompanied her.

GLORIA ESTEFAN

On March 20, 1990, tragedy struck when Gloria's tour bus was hit from behind.

The bus driver was hurt but escaped serious injury. Nayib was thrown to the floor, and Emilio found him with a broken collarbone, lying under a mountain of purses, books, and bags that had been thrown around in the crash. Gloria was in excruciating pain. She could not move, but she was relieved to see that her husband and son were alive.

Originally, Gloria was told that it would be a long wait for the ambulance to get to her because the road was blocked. The nearest hospital was in Scranton, about an hour away. But the police sent a helicopter to rescue them.

Gloria had to lie in agonizing pain for more than an hour waiting for a helicopter to reach the bus. She was able to control the pain because her son was there. She didn't want him to know how much pain she was in. "I was forced to really keep a lot of control," Gloria remembers, "because I didn't want [Nayib] freaking out. There was chaos on that bus. And I still remember as a child that if you were to see your parents lose control in any situation, it would really be a very traumatic thing, because you always think adults have a grip on everything. And I didn't want him to feel that we had lost that grip for him, so he helped me hang on."

The paramedics finally arrived. Gloria had to be removed through the windshield because the door to the bus was only inches away from a steep, icy slope. She was strapped to a stretcher and taken to the hospital. The doctors confirmed what she had suspected: her back was broken. It was her worst nightmare come true. She thought her career as a performer was over.

Gloria's vertebrae in the middle of her back were broken. The doctors told her about a new type of surgery that could repair her back and allow her to walk again. The surgery was a risk, however, because if it failed, she could be permanently paralyzed. On March 23, the doctors at the Hospital for Joint Diseases in New York City performed the operation. They put steel rods in Gloria's back, and it was a complete success.

It took many months of rest and therapy for Gloria to recover. She received thousands of cards and letters from fans all over the country. She was thankful that she had such support.

In September 1990, Gloria made her first public appearance after the accident. She was in a film clip that was taped for the Jerry Lewis Labor Day Telethon for the Muscular Dystrophy Association. She was not yet able to perform, but she promised her fans she would be back.

During the time that she was confined, Gloria wrote several songs that she would record on her next album. She asked Jon Secada to help her with several of these songs. Together they wrote "Coming Out of the Dark" and "Can't Forget You." The two songs were released on her next album, *Into the Light,* and they both became hits.

▼▼▼▼▼▼
It took many months of rest and therapy for Gloria to recover. She received thousands of cards and letters from fans all over the country.
▲▲▲▲▲▲

GLORIA ESTEFAN

Gloria returned to performing in January 1991 when she appeared at the American Music Awards. In March, she launched a yearlong worldwide tour to promote *Into the Light*.

To commemorate Gloria's success, Epic Records released *Gloria Estefan's Greatest Hits* in November 1992. "It's been my dream to one day be able to create a greatest hits album," she had said at the time. "Not just a compilation, but a culmination of years of hard work and successful collaborations." The album featured ten of her top-ten hits, plus four brand-new recordings. One of the new recordings was "Always Tomorrow," a song written for and inspired by the victims of Hurricane Andrew. Gloria and Emilio donated all of the artist and songwriting royalties received from "Always Tomorrow" to the Hurricane Relief Fund. They raised nearly $3 million for the victims of the hurricane.

Gloria's *Into the Light* tour was the first after her bus accident.

In 1993, the group released *Mi Tierra*, an all-Spanish tribute to their homeland, which they had dreamed of doing for years. The lead single and title track is a celebration of music and people in Latin America. "My fans are hearing me sing on this album in a way they've never heard before," said Gloria. "That's how I did it when I first sang when I was nine and my audience was my grandmother." The album yielded four top-ten singles, including three number one hits. The album was a success in the United States, Spain, and Latin America.

In May of 1993, Gloria visited Ellis Island, where she was presented with the Ellis Island Congressional Medal of Honor. It was a moment of supreme significance for her. The ceremony acknowledged the fact that when she travels to the corners of the world, Gloria Estefan is an ambassador for all Americans, and that as a daughter of Cuban immigrants, she also represents the millions of Hispanics, who, like her family, have made the United States their home.

There was more good news for the Estefans in 1994. On December 5, 1994, Gloria gave birth to a baby girl. Named Emily Marie Estefan Fajardo, she weighed 6 pounds 14 ounces and was 19 inches long. Emily was a dream come true for Gloria and Emilio. Before the bus accident in 1990, the couple had discussed plans for having another child. The accident changed all that. Not only did it take Gloria a while to recover, but the accident had left one of her fallopian tubes injured, and that had to be corrected before she was able to conceive. The baby appeared with the whole family on *Oprah Winfrey*. Gloria planned to take a year or two off from traveling to be with her new baby. In the meantime, among his many other projects, Emilio kept as busy as ever, producing material that was released for the Disney movie *Pocahontas*.

▼▼▼▼▼▼
In May of 1993, Gloria visited Ellis Island, where she was presented with the Ellis Island Congressional Medal of Honor.
▲▲▲▲▲▲

GLORIA ESTEFAN

"Cuba needs to be a free and democratic society where its citizens are allowed to vote for whomever they wish," she states, calling for an end to the dictatorship.

In September 1995, Gloria released *Abriendo Puertas* (Opening Doors), another Spanish-language album. Baby Emily was by her mother's side while Gloria recorded the new album. Emilio said, "This was more of a musical homage to Latinos. We brought a lot of different people from Latin America to play on the album—especially from Colombia—because I was thinking if we were going to do another Spanish-language album, we should pay tribute to Latin America with a record that hopefully will make Latins feel closer to each other."

"The really good thing about Gloria," says Frank Ceraolo, director of marketing for Epic Records, "is that she has transcended the lines defining a pop artist. The domestic fans really like her because it's Gloria, and it doesn't matter what language she is singing."

Though she had not resumed extensive touring after Emily was born, Gloria and Emilio did travel to the U.S. camp in Guantánamo in September 1995. A U.S. Navy DC-9 took their band and movie star Andy Garcia with them to visit 15,000 Cuban men who were awaiting their delivery to the United States after they defected in 1994. (Guantánamo is a U.S. camp on the island of Cuba where the U.S. Navy is protecting thousands of Cuban refugees who want to leave Cuba but cannot gain legal entry to the U.S. at the moment.)

Gloria gave a large concert, amplified one hundred times, at the edge of Guantánamo Bay.

GLORIA ESTEFAN

She gave the concert with no promotional fan-
fare and no media coverage. She did it to show
her support for the refugees and to let them
know they are not forgotten. It was difficult for
Gloria to be back in Cuba. "Performing *Mi Tierra*
was so emotional," she remembers. "When we
played *Abriendo Puertas*, they joined in after one
time. It was sweet but sad. Miami is my town,
America is my country, but Cuba is
also *mi tierra*." To this day, Gloria
does not make a secret of her feelings toward the Cuban government
or its dictator, Fidel Castro. "Cuba
needs to be a free and democratic
society where its citizens are allowed to vote for whomever they
wish," she states, calling for an end
to the dictatorship. "The day that
happens, there is going to be a big
party. In fact, I'll throw a huge party
myself!"

In October 1995, Gloria performed in Rome with a 62-member
orchestra for Pope John Paul II. "I was told the
Pope had been watching me for some time and
wanted me to sing at the Vatican," said Gloria.
Then, on December 12, Gloria performed for
President Bill Clinton and First Lady Hillary
Rodham Clinton at a Washington, D.C., Christmas special.

Gloria's first English-language album since
1991, *Destiny*, was released June 4, 1996. A

It doesn't matter to
Gloria's fans what
language she sings in.

GLORIA ESTEFAN

single from her new album, "Reach," was released in March. Emily accompanied her mother

Gloria with Emilio and baby Emily

on her tour, which began with a special performance on July 18 at the 1996 Olympic games in Atlanta, Georgia, where she sang a song she recorded especially for the Olympics.

Gloria has been approached for several movie roles, but she has not felt ready to tackle the Hollywood scene just yet. "I've had offers to do movies, but I'm not interested. In fact I was offered the part of the female Hispanic attorney in the film *Disclosure*, but I felt I wasn't ready for it. Right now, I just want to concentrate on my children and watch them grow up into happy, healthy adults," she said.

The Estefans' home on one of Miami Beach's islands is always filled with fun. For Gloria's birthday in 1994, her friends and relatives sneaked into their garden dressed as a mariachi band. They brought a cow along with them, because Gloria is fond of cows (and all animals in general). The group was going to sing under the balcony. "I heard a noise and almost called the police," recalls Gloria. "I thought they were intruders."

GLORIA ESTEFAN

The Estefans have overcome many obstacles in their lives to achieve the success they both have earned. Gloria is ever thankful she was able to recover from her accident and return to the performing she loves. "I speak of being reborn in many ways. I was always a thankful person," she says, "because I did go through some difficult things, but you tend to forget and get caught up in petty stuff. The bottom line is that we're here for each other."

Gloria is fond of all animals.

SELECTED DISCOGRAPHY

Renacer	Discos CBS International	1981
Otra Vez	Discos CBS International	1981
Rio	Discos CBS International	1982
Eyes of Innocence	Epic Records	1984
Primitive Love	Epic Records	1985
Let it Loose	Epic Records	1987
Cuts Both Ways	Epic Records	1989
Into the Light	Epic Records	1991
Greatest Hits	Epic Records	1992
Mi Tierra (My Land)	Epic Records	1993
Abriendo Puertas (Opening Doors)	Epic Records	1995
Destiny	Epic Records	1996

34

FERNANDO CUZA

Baseball Agent
1957-

"**W**e are very fortunate to live in a country where everyone has the opportunity to reach his or her dreams. Even if you are at the point in your life where you may not realize your full potential, keep working toward your dreams. Dedicate yourself to improving in every way through your studies, through athletics, through the arts, or wherever your strengths and interests lie.

"Always apply yourself with enthusiasm, whether it is in your school work, team sports, or your relationships with people. Your likelihood of success will be increased by that simple attitude alone."

Fernando Cuza, as told to Barbara Marvis, April 1996

BIO HIGHLIGHTS

- Born April 6, 1957, in Santiago de Cuba; mother: Isabel Luisa Durand del Castillo; father: Rafael Luis Cuza-Diaz
- Came to the United States at age two; grew up in Miami, Florida
- In early 1970s, met and became friends with Angelo Dundee, the famous boxing trainer, who influenced his decision to pursue a sports-related career
- 1976, was graduated from North Miami High
- 1980, earned B.A. in business administration from Florida State University
- 1980-1984, worked for Northwestern Mutual Life Insurance Company
- 1984-1987, joined Coordinated Sports as a sports agent
- 1987-present, baseball agent for Speakers of Sport
- Currently: married to Kristi Huoni; they have three daughters: Ashlee, Kalynne, and Kristin; they live in Chicago, Illinois

In January 1959, when Fern was only two, Fidel Castro gained power in Cuba and announced that his new government would align itself with the Soviet Union.

FERNANDO CUZA

When Fern Cuza played linebacker for the North Miami High Pioneers back in 1975, he knew he wanted to pursue a career in sports. Exactly what form that career would take was very much in question. But that didn't bother the 5-foot-10, 175-pound Cuza, who was named a top athlete in his junior year. In an early game in October 1975, Fernando made twelve unassisted tackles and assisted on five others. His coach was pleased that Fernando had become much stronger between his sophomore and junior years. Fern liked to lift weights, and he worked out regularly at the Fifth Street Gym. Maybe he would become a famous professional football player someday. But it turned out that Fern would rather be the low-key force behind the stars: today he is a baseball agent, representing and negotiating for Hispanic baseball players from many corners of the world.

Fernando Enrique Cuza was born on April 6, 1957, in Santiago de Cuba. He is the second son of Rafael Luis Cuza-Diaz and Isabel Luisa Durand del Castillo, both natives of Cuba. He has one brother, Rafael Cuza-Durand, who was born on September 7, 1955.

In Cuba, Fern's father's family owned a 10,000-acre sugarcane ranch, which was named Regina, after his grandmother. His mother's family owned the Rum Castillo Company, which was later purchased by Bacardi Industries. The family was very well off and enjoyed a life of luxury and leisure. Fern's parents were divorced when he was quite small, and he did not see his father much when he was growing up. But this was not the biggest disruption to his life of leisure. In January 1959, when Fern was only two, Fidel Castro gained power in Cuba and announced that his new government would align itself with the Soviet Union. According to communist principles, individuals could not own businesses or other profit-making entities. All the businesses were seized and given to the govern-

ment. Fern's family lost nearly everything they owned. The Cuzas came to the United States in 1960 with nothing. Only his paternal grandparents had been able to leave Cuba with anything of value.

The family split up. His father went to New

Fern (right) with his brother Rafael, taken in 1960 in Santiago de Cuba

York, remarried, and worked in the construction business. His mother, brother, and Fern went to Miami to stay with his mother's sister Yvonne and her husband Eduardo.

A divorced woman with two small children, no understanding of the English language, and

He was hit with all the cultural bias at once on his first day of kindergarten when he was enrolled at St. Rose of Lima in Miami Shores in 1963. He could not speak one word of English.

FERNANDO CUZA

no skills to support herself faced incredible odds in a new culture, a new country, a new homeland. But Fern's mother had the strength and courage she needed to begin again—and to succeed. As soon as she got to Miami, she enrolled at Barry College and studied English and nursing. When she got her first job, the family moved to their own two-bedroom home. Two months later, Fern's grandparents were allowed to leave Cuba and they came to live with them. His mother was hired at the Cohen Clinic to work with many of the Spanish-speaking immigrants. She worked six days and 50 hours a week to support all of them. Fern remembers that Sundays were her only days off, and the entire family would spend Sundays together at the beach.

But there were more obstacles to be overcome. Cuba is a multiracial, multicolored society that has little or no prejudice. Members of all ethnic and racial backgrounds live together, marry, and share a common culture. In the 1960s, Miami was often a spot of racial unrest, as many Cubans chose Miami to be their home. But where Fern's family chose to settle, there was not a large Latin population. Most of the Cuban population settled in southwest Miami. Fern's family settled in north Miami, because when his aunt and uncle moved there, they had felt those schools were better. But this created even bigger problems for Fernando. He was hit with all the cultural bias at once on his first day of kindergarten when he was enrolled at St. Rose of

FERNANDO CUZA

Lima in Miami Shores in 1963. He could not speak one word of English. Though his mother was learning English so that she could communicate in her job, she spoke Spanish to Fern and Rafael at home. Fern had to learn English at school. "My parents did what they could for me by bringing me to the United States," Fern says, "but it was beyond their abilities to smooth my way into the public school system. I soon learned that any success I had would be the success I made for myself."

St. Rose of Lima is a private Catholic school in Miami. Fern's grandmother (his father's mother, Regina Diaz) helped with the tuition because she wanted to make sure her grandchildren got a good education. His teacher took extra time with Fern to help him learn to speak English, and by second grade he was able to communicate well, even though he still spoke with a Spanish accent. Fern enjoyed math, science, and physical education most in school, and even though he learned to speak English rather quickly, he says that reading was always tough for him. For this reason, he was never more than an average student all through school. If he had difficulties with anything in school, especially reading, he couldn't ask his mother because she couldn't read English, either. This meant that he never heard stories read to him in English at home, and it restricted the rate at which he could learn other things.

▼▼▼▼▼

"I soon learned that any success I had would be the success I made for myself."

▲▲▲▲▲▲

FERNANDO CUZA

Fern's grandmother, Regina Diaz (front center), is shown here with her brothers and sisters behind her, Fern (to the right) and Fern's wife, Kristi (to the left); taken in Miami, 1983

At first, Fern found it a little tough to make friends at school. It is difficult to be friendly to people when you can't speak the same language. But as he learned English, he found it easier to find friends. In the lower grades, the children had very few preconceived ideas about Cubans, and they liked Fern because he was Fern. But he remembers once being invited to a friend's house to play after school. His friend had an older brother who immediately quizzed Fern on his ancestry. The next day, this little boy didn't want to be Fern's friend anymore.

Fern stayed at St. Rose of Lima through eighth grade. He always loved sports. In sixth, seventh,

FERNANDO CUZA

and eighth grades, he played basketball, baseball, and football at the Miami Shores recreation center. He also played basketball for St. Rose, which was the only sports team available at school. Two very good friends of his, Tim and Greg Stead, attended St. Rose and played many sports with him. Tim was Fern's age and Greg was two years older. Fern remembers a tragic accident that occurred when he was in seventh grade and Greg was in ninth grade. Greg, a star athlete, was playing varsity football as a freshman. On opening day, he was making a tackle

Fern played basketball for St. Rose of Lima. He is #51 in the middle row; 1971

when his helmet slid off his head and he broke his neck. Greg was paralyzed from the neck down.

Fern (left) with Greg (center) and Tim Stead (right), 1994

▼▼▼▼▼▼

"Greg taught me how unimportant material things are."

▲▲▲▲▲▲

"Everyone looked up to Greg," remembers Fern, "not only because of his athletic ability, but because of his attitude." Greg was given a slim chance of surviving and eventually spent eight and a half months in a Houston, Texas, rehabilitation center. Fern recalls the events.

"Greg's brother, four other friends, and I put all of our money together and drove to Houston to spend ten days visiting Greg. Up until that time, no one had been allowed to see him. We hardly recognized him. He had lost one hundred pounds and was connected to a respirator and other machines and tubes. When I walked into his room, I couldn't even speak. Greg said to me, 'Hey, don't worry about this. I'm going to have a good attitude and I'm going to get through it.' When Greg got home from rehab, he finished high school, learned to drive his own wheelchair, finished college, and started his own business. What a tremendous inspiration he is. Greg taught me how unimportant material things are, and that everything I had longed for up to that point because we were so poor didn't really matter. It was then that I realized that the things that come to us for free—our health, our friends, our family, and our faith in God—are the only things of true value; they should be the most carefully guarded and protected. Material things can all be replaced."

In 1972, Fern went to live with his grandmother, Regina Diaz, to keep her company; she had just moved to the Miami area. Though she lived only about two miles away from his mother, her house was in another school district. He enrolled at Edison Intermediate School for ninth grade, where he played junior varsity football. The next year, he went back to live with his mother and spent the next three years at North Miami High. As a sophomore, he played varsity football. When Fern reached high school, he gave up playing baseball and basketball to make time for work. "I never had enough spending money," Fern remembers. "If I wanted money for clothes or other things, I had to earn it myself. Between working and schoolwork, there wasn't enough time to play basketball and baseball anymore. I continued to play football because I enjoyed that the most. Football got all the attention in Miami. I never worked during the football season."

While Fern was in high school, he had a friend named Terri Dundee. One day, she introduced Fern to her parents, Helen and Angelo Dundee. Her father, Angelo, is a famous boxing

"If I wanted money for clothes or other things, I had to earn it myself. Between working and schoolwork, there wasn't enough time to play basketball and baseball anymore."

trainer: he has trained fourteen world champions, including Muhammad Ali and Sugar Ray Leonard. The Dundees became like Fern's second family. Angelo became the father he never really had. "During the summers when I wasn't

Fern (center) with sports reporter Howard Cosell (left) and boxing trainer Angelo Dundee (right)

working in the evenings," Fern recalls, "I would hang around the Fifth Street Gym in South Beach and watch him work. He is a great motivator and he always knows what to tell an athlete to make him give his best performance instead of only telling him what he wants to hear. He demands a fighter's respect, and he showed me that the very best business and personal relationships are based on mutual respect.

"It was Angelo who opened the world of sports to me. I knew I wanted to have a future in sports, and Angelo taught me many things. I liked the way he handled the press and how he treated the fighters. He never wanted to be the center of attention. He always focused on the athlete and never on himself. In his mind, the fighter was the show. He has made a real difference in the lives of the athletes he has trained—not only by the fights he helped them win, but in their personal lives as well. He taught them to project a positive image, to act responsibly, and to respect the fact that they are role models.

"Helen and Angelo helped me with my personal life, giving me advice and reminding me that although I might be broke, I wasn't poor, and that whatever I had lost when we left Cuba could be regained by my hard work. Angelo was the best man at my wedding, and we still have a close relationship today. We visit each other whenever we can."

Fern with Boots (center) and Jeff Manchester (right)

Fern was graduated from North Miami High in 1976. He then went on to spend a year at Wittenberg University in Springfield, Ohio, on a grant-in-aid program. There he met Jeff Manchester, who was from Sidney, Ohio. Fern was away from home for the first time, and he was too far from Florida to return there for the weekends. Jeff and his parents, Chuck and Boots, welcomed

FERNANDO CUZA

him into their family. They always took the time to include Fern in all their family events. "They provided me with a different view of life in the United States than I had ever experienced. They were the perfect white-collar, upper-middle-class, loving and devoted family. In short, I thought they were living the American dream. In many ways, I modeled my own family after theirs. I was best man at Jeff's wedding, and I kept in close contact with Chuck until he died several years ago. Boots is now 'Granma Boots' to my children."

Fern with his mother on his wedding day, 1983

Fern enjoyed Wittenberg University, but he found he could not handle the financial end. Though his tuition was completely paid for, he had to raise money for airfare to get home several times a year. The school and the surrounding community did not have many opportunities for Fern to get a job, and he finally decided that he would be better off going to college closer to home. In 1977, Fern enrolled at Florida State University, which was about an eight-hour car ride from his home. He took out a student loan and worked as a college agent for Northwestern Mutual Insurance Company. In 1980, Fern was awarded a bachelor's degree in business administration. After graduation, he continued to work for Northwestern because the flexible hours allowed him the freedom to pursue aspects of his as-yet undefined sports career. He did not have to report to an office for any set number of hours, and he could work weekends and nights if he wanted.

While he was at Florida State, Fern met Kristi Huoni in chemistry class. They dated for nearly six years. Kristi graduated from Florida State in 1982 with a Bachelor's of Science in Nursing. On March 26, 1983, Fern and Kristi were married in Panama City Beach, Florida. Their first daughter, Ashlee, was born later that year, on December 20, 1983, in Tallahassee.

In 1980, when Ronald Reagan became President, he passed the Caribbean Basin Initiative, which was designed to provide financial aid to the islands in the Caribbean Sea. It was not a gift of financial aid, but a measure that allowed the islands to export goods to the United States without adding duty (additional taxes). This provided a lot of opportunity for U.S. manufacturers to do business in the Dominican Republic. Fernando started making trips to the Dominican Republic with friends he had met through Northwestern Mutual who wanted to pursue business opportunities there. Through Northwestern, Fern met Bill Crona, an accountant from the accounting firm Law, Redd, and Crona in Tallahassee. Bill asked Fern to accompany him and his clients and act as an interpreter, since Bill and his

Fern made many trips to the Dominican Republic in an informal capacity, just to help out. Over the years, he met a lot of people and developed a lot of contacts there and in Puerto Rico.

"I chose this career because I saw a tremendous need for Spanish-speaking agents to represent Hispanic players."

clients spoke no Spanish. For the next several years, Fern made many trips to the Dominican Republic in an informal capacity, just to help out. Over the years, he met a lot of people and developed a lot of contacts there and in Puerto Rico. On one of his trips, Fern met Jorge Bournigal, who was the number one sports announcer in the Dominican Republic. He and Jorge found out that they were distant relatives, and they became good friends. Jorge always took Fern to baseball games whenever Fern was in town. Pretty soon, Fern knew many of the ballplayers in the Dominican Republic. Because he is bilingual, Fern was able to help some of the players with advice on their careers with ball teams in the United States. Fern soon found that he loved baseball, and he loved talking to the ballplayers and the media and helping whenever he could.

From 1980 to 1984, while he kept his flexible job with Northwestern Mutual, Fern continued to network and to make contacts in the islands. In 1984, another agent at Northwestern Mutual in Chicago, Harry Hoopis, heard about Fern's trips to the islands. He had just started a sports agency called Coordinated Sports, and he contacted Fern to see if he might be interested in helping with the new business. Harry and Fern traveled to the Dominican Republic and spoke to many of the players. They saw great potential in the Hispanic market. "I knew that within a few years, I could be a major influence in the Hispanic market," recalls Fern.

Fern finally found his sports career—or maybe it found him. Since he had such a love of sports, he thought he could help protect the interests of others who chose to make sports their career. "I chose this career because I saw a tremendous need for Spanish-speaking agents to represent Hispanic players. I felt that I could make a difference in the lives of the Hispanic players by representing them with honesty and integrity. I feel a strong kinship with many of the young players who come from poverty and work so hard to achieve success. I am rewarded by the confidence they place in me and how I become a part of their lives." The first major-league star that Fern represented was not from the Dominican Republic, however. In 1984, Fern represented Teddy Higuera from Mexico, who became one of baseball's top pitchers.

In 1985, 1986, and 1987, Fern spent the winters in the Dominican Republic and Puerto Rico developing business contacts. In 1985, he moved his family to Chicago to pursue his career as a full-time sports agent. In 1986, Fern went to San Juan, Puerto Rico, to look for talent and to recruit players for Coordinated Sports. There he met Bob Gilhooley and Jim Bronner, who had started a similar agency called Speakers of Sport. Their agency represented only baseball players, and Fern could see that the direction that Speakers of Sport was taking was more along the lines

▼▼▼▼▼

"I am rewarded by the confidence they place in me and how I become a part of their lives."

▲▲▲▲▲▲

FERNANDO CUZA

Teddy Higuera (far right), who pitched for the Milwaukee Brewers, was the first major-league star that Fern represented. Shown here with Teddy (from left to right): Teddy's wife, Lulu Higuera, Fern, Kristi, Fern's daughters Ashlee and Kalynne

of what he wanted. He enjoyed baseball most of all, and in 1987 Fern decided to join Speakers of Sport. All of the players that Fern had represented at Coordinated Sports decided to follow him to his new job.

Speakers of Sport represents both major-league and minor-league baseball players. Many minor-league clients are referred by major-league clients or by retired players who have moved into managing or coaching positions. Because Speakers of Sport does not charge minor-league players a fee, the firm tries very hard to work for players who understand the value of the time and effort devoted to them and the quality of the advice provided to them when they are on the minor-league level. It is each agent's job to devote all of his creative and intellectual energies to helping each player achieve his fullest potential at every level of his career.

At Speakers of Sport, there are five agents working for approximately 130 baseball players. Jim Bronner is an attorney with experience as a litigator, as well as having taught law for ten years as a member of the faculty of Northwestern University School of Law. Bob Gilhooley's background is in financial investments. Bob also played professional baseball for five years with

The Speakers of Sport organization (left to right, back row): Bob Greenwald, Fern, Dan Durst, Jim Bronner, Bob Gilhooley, Pat Rooney, Pete Smith, Brian David; (front): Laura, Marty, and Kristie

A first-year rookie player is often paid only $5,000 a year. The players accept such small salaries for the chance that they will play major-league ball for much higher salaries sometime in the future.

FERNANDO CUZA

the Detroit Tigers and the Oakland Athletics. Pat Rooney joined the company in 1985. He, too, was a professional baseball player and had spent seven years playing for the Montreal Expos, the New York Yankees, and the Toronto Blue Jays. Brian David and Fern both joined the firm in 1987. Brian, like Jim Bronner, is an attorney. Before joining Speakers of Sport, Brian had extensive experience in salary arbitration and contract negotiation. Since Fern is bilingual, he was a natural choice to represent the firm's Hispanic players. Bob Greenwald, an attorney, and Peter Smith, an accountant, also work for the firm, where they help the players with their financial planning and prepare their federal, state, and, in many cases, foreign income tax returns.

A baseball player will hire an agent for many reasons. The agent is paid a percentage of the player's salary for negotiating the best contract for the player, for representing him in arbitration if he is eligible, and for negotiating product endorsements and appearances.

Baseball works very differently than the other major sports, which is why Speakers of Sport prefers to represent only baseball players. Football and basketball teams draw their players from college teams, which act as minor leagues for those sports. Often, these players are offered multimillion-dollar contracts right out of college. But baseball teams finance their own minor leagues. A team can have several minor leagues to draw talent from, but the players on these minor leagues are paid a very small salary. In fact, a first-year rookie player is often paid only $5,000 a year. The players accept such small salaries for the chance that they will play major-league ball for much higher salaries sometime in the future. Each team has its own salary schedule, and a team can keep a player on its minor-league teams for many years. Sometimes, a player will think he has broken through to the major league, only to be sent back to a triple-A team several weeks later. It takes a lot of work and consistently good playing to break through to the major leagues and stay there.

Once a player has been called up to a major-league team, he is paid a set salary according to the team's schedule. The minimum salary for the first year in the major leagues is approximately $109,000. Second- and third-year players can expect to earn between $109,000 and $500,000, depending on the team they play for and their performance from the prior year. By this time, the player can start paying off all the debt he has accumulated from working for such a small salary over the years in the minor leagues.

Arbitration is a legal process available to major-league players with three years of experience. Arbitration is used when a player feels that there is a great disparity between the value of the contract that his team offers him and what he feels he is worth based on his service time and performance. If the team and the player cannot

▼▼▼▼▼▼
Once a player has been called up to a major-league team, he is paid a set salary according to the team's schedule.
▲▲▲▲▲▲

reach an agreement, the team is notified of the player's intent to seek arbitration. Then both the team and the player, through his agents, submit a salary number. The player's agents and the team prepare a case supporting their submission. The case is then presented to the arbitrator. Based on the arguments of both sides, the arbitrator makes a binding decision in favor of one of the parties. If the case is strong, and if the agents have done their job, the decision will be made in favor of the player.

Rafael Palmeiro is the godfather of Kalynne, Fern's second daughter. Photo 1989

In 1992, Rafael Palmeiro was playing for the Texas Rangers. The Rangers offered him a $2.35 million salary for his fourth year on the team. Rafael thought he was worth much more. Speakers of Sport asked the arbitrator to award Rafael a $3.85 million salary. The difference between what the team offered and Rafael's request was $1.5 million, one of the largest spreads in baseball history. Speakers of Sport won the higher salary for Rafael. Having an agency with experience, especially in arbitration, could have a tremendous impact on a player's compensation!

After six years on a major-league team, a player may declare himself a free agent and may entertain offers from any ball club. The contract that the player will sign as a free agent depends

Fern with Cecil Fielder in the Dominican Republic, Nov. 1995. Cecil was the 1989-90 homerun champ for the Detroit Tigers.

on many factors. The most important factor is the player's ability to help his team win games. Other factors that may improve the player's bargaining position are his ability to draw fans and the number of teams that are interested in the player at the time he declares himself a free agent. When many teams are interested in a player, it is particularly important that he be represented by an agency with experience in negotiating free-agent contracts.

Moises Alou with Kalynne, 1995

Speakers of Sport has negotiated some of the largest free-agent contracts in baseball. Among them are Cecil Fielder's five-year contract with the Detroit Tigers for $36 million; Juan Gonzalez's five-year contract for $31 million, plus $14 million in options for years six and seven with the Texas Rangers; Rafael Palmeiro of the Baltimore Orioles for $30 million for five years; Ramon Martinez's $15 million three-year contract with a $5 million option for the fourth year with the Los Angeles Dodgers; Larry Walker's $22 million for four years plus a $5 million option for the fifth year with the Colorado Rockies; and Andres Galarraga's $17 million four-year contract, also with the Rockies.

Speakers of Sport represents many other Latino ballplayers, including Moises Alou (Montreal Expos), Pedro Astacio (Los Angeles Dodgers), Rafael Bournigal (Oakland Athletics), Leo Gomez (Chicago Cubs), Alex Gonzalez (Toronto

FERNANDO CUZA

Blue Jays), Pedro Martinez (Montreal Expos), Jamie Navarro (Chicago Cubs), Mariano Rivera (New York Yankees), Ruben Rivera (New York Yankees), Mel Rojas (Montreal Expos), Ismael Valdes (Los Angeles Dodgers), and Luis Sojo (Seattle Mariners). Fern enjoys helping the young players develop their careers. He enjoys being a part of their lives both on and off the ball field. For some of the ballplayers he represents, their success on a professional team is like living a fairy tale. Such is the case with Ramon Martinez, who now pitches for the Los Angeles Dodgers.

Ramon Martinez, All-Star pitcher with the L.A. Dodgers, and his aunt Gloria Martinez at Fern's home, summer 1995

"When I first met Ramon in 1987, he lived in a shack in the Dominican Republic," remembers Fern. "There were holes where windows used to be, and the ramshackle hut had no indoor plumbing. But once Ramon made the major leagues, he bought his family a brand-new house." With the money that Ramon now earns, he can buy new houses for many people. But Fern says his life in the Dominican Republic does not really resemble what we are used to in the United States.

Ramon grew up poor, the son of a school maintenance worker. Ramon and his two brothers were incredibly thin because there was never enough food to eat. Their house barely supplied a roof over their heads. In the backyard, there was an outhouse. Near his house, the women washed clothes in big tubs outside. Children without shoes, and many without shirts, gathered every afternoon to play baseball with a thin stick and a rubber ball. Many afternoons, they could find no ball to play with. A dozen or more children would search the outfield weeds for a ball so that they could begin their game. This is where Ramon grew up, hoping that someday someone would give him a baseball to play with. In fact, he dreamed that he could see a real baseball game someday, and that one of the players would toss him a game ball. He never dared to dream, however, that one day he would be the one to toss the game ball.

Evilo Jiminez was the Dodgers' Dominican Republic scout who invited Ramon to try out at camp. At age 15, when Ramon left the shack he lived in to show up for the Dodgers tryout at Campos Las Palmas Academy, he weighed 135 pounds, he had no socks, and his cap was torn. He was so thin, he could not throw a ball faster than 80 miles per hour. No one at the Dodgers wanted him.

Ramon spent a year at the Dodgers academy, and in 1984, he pitched for the Dominican Republic baseball team in the Olympics at Dodger Stadium. Though he was still very thin, he had great determination. He was signed by the Dodgers, but his first two pro seasons were disasters. He was 8-9 with a 3.98 earned run average (ERA) and nearly as many walks—86—as strikeouts—120. And he was losing weight because of all

At age 15, when Ramon left the shack he lived in to show up for the Dodgers tryout at Campos Las Palmas Academy, he weighed 135 pounds, he had no socks, and his cap was torn.

Ramon thought he had made the major-league team in 1989 after he shut out the Atlanta Braves, winning the first game of a doubleheader. But the Dodgers did not ask him to stay.

the exercise! In the winter of 1986, after the season was over, Ramon was ordered to spend more time at the Dodgers academy or at the homes of the coaches so he could eat better meals. A lifetime of bad nutrition made it difficult for Ramon to gain weight. When he returned to the Dominican Republic for visits, he did not eat well. By the spring of 1987, Ramon could throw the ball faster than 90 miles per hour. That season, he went 16-5 with a 2.17 ERA for Vero Beach. He was protected on the Dodgers' roster and he was pitching in Los Angeles at the end of 1988. But he still had to find a way to break into the Dodger pitching rotation.

Ramon thought he had made the major-league team in 1989 after he shut out the Atlanta Braves, winning the first game of a doubleheader. But the Dodgers did not ask him to stay. They sent him back to triple-A in Albuquerque. He was crushed. It was the 1990 ball season before Ramon was able to make his mark. That was the season he won twenty games.

That year, he was chosen to pitch in the All-Star game. The fans choose who plays on the All-Star teams. But it is the managers of the team who won the previous year's World Series who choose the pitchers for the game. On July 9, 1990, in the All-Star game in Chicago's Wrigley Field, Ramon found himself facing power-hitter José Canseco. There were runners on first and second and two out in the third inning of a scoreless game. On one pitch, Ramon brushed

Canseco back. Then he fooled him into a lunging miss. Then, after running the count to 3-2, he threw several fastballs that Canseco fouled off. Finally, Ramon threw a pitch that Canseco turned into a very weak grounder, which ended the inning.

In 1990, Ramon earned nearly $150,000. In 1995, Fern and Speakers of Sport helped Ramon sign a $15 million three-year deal with the Dodgers. "I feel I made a difference in his life," Fern says. "To see a player grow professionally and financially gives me the greatest satisfaction."

Ramon can now buy anything he wants. But he likes his roots in the Dominican Republic. "I don't want to get too far away from those days," says Ramon. "I want to stay close to where I'm from. If you see me here [in the Dominican Republic], you know that I am not that different from them."

The children in the Dominican Republic still rush up to Ramon's house when he is home. "Ramon! Ramon!" they yell. "Come out and play."

"They always want me to pitch," he says. And, of course, they want to be like him. Ramon played in the same park the children play ball in today. If Ramon can pitch for the Dodgers, they have hope that they can, too.

Fern is proud of the way he can help many players through his association with Speakers of Sport. But one tale he especially likes to tell is the story of Andres Galarraga. "I like this story,"

"To see a player grow professionally and financially gives me the greatest satisfaction."

FERNANDO CUZA

Fern says, "because Andres has a lot of courage, and I'm glad I was around to help him when he needed me."

Andres Galarraga (originally from Venezuela) had been with the Montreal Expos since 1987. But for the 1992 season, Montreal traded him to the St. Louis Cardinals. During the third game of that season, Andres broke his hand. As a result, he had a very poor season, and St. Louis decided not to sign him again at the end of the year. A lot of people in baseball thought that Andres was finished.

"But Andres did not give up on himself," says Fern. "In 1993, there were two new expansion teams, the Colorado Rockies and the Florida Marlins. Don Baylor had been Andres's hitting coach in St. Louis, and he became the manager of the Colorado Rockies. He still believed in Andres,

Fern, Andres Galarraga, and Moises Alou enjoy a fishing trip, 1995

and so did everyone at our firm. Speakers of Sport had a very good relationship with Bob Gebhard, the general manager of the Rockies, and together we were able to find a spot for Andres on the Rockies. We structured his contract so that there was very little risk in it for

Colorado. Andres was paid a salary ($600,000), but he was given lots of opportunities to earn bonus money if he did well. Things started out well for Andres that season. But in July, he was hurt again when a second baseman, Roberto Mejia, ran into him, injuring his knee. It was nearly a disaster. We sent Andres to see a specialist for a second opinion. The specialist, Dr.

Snorkeling in Aruba, 1992

FERNANDO CUZA

Richard Steadman of the Steadman-Hawkins clinic, worked with Andres and made him a special brace so that he could return to play as soon as possible, postponing any surgery until after the season was over. When Andres finally made it back into the lineup, he picked up where he left off and won the National League Batting Champion title for 1993! Speakers of Sport was able to sign a four-year $17 million deal for Andres after that."

FERNANDO CUZA

Today, Speakers of Sport is one of the most established firms in baseball, and Fernando is happy that he has been able to define a sports career he enjoys so much. The only drawback he sees to his career is the travel: he has to be away from his family too much. But he says his wife, Kristi, and his three children, Ashlee, Kalynne, and Kristin, are very understanding and supportive. They love doing things as a family, including fishing, scuba diving, snorkeling, making artwork, and listening to all types of music. For Fern, there is no doubt about what he'll be doing ten or twenty years from now. "I'll be a baseball agent then as I am now," he says. "I love this life."

Fern and Ashlee play baseball together

ROSIE PEREZ

Actress, Dancer, Choreographer
1964-

"The racism, the sexism, I never let it be my problem. It's their problem. If I see a door comin' my way, I'm knockin' it down. And if I can't knock down the door, I'm sliding through the window. I'll never let it stop me from what I want to do.**"**

Rosie Perez, to *Entertainment Weekly*, November 5, 1993

BIO HIGHLIGHTS

- Born 1964 in Brooklyn, New York; mother: Lydia; father: Ismael Serrano Perez
- Attended Los Angeles City College and West Los Angeles College
- Danced on the TV show *Soul Train*
- 1989, starred in her first motion picture, Spike Lee's *Do the Right Thing*, with no previous acting experience
- 1992, starred in *White Men Can't Jump*
- 1993, starred in *Fearless* with Jeff Bridges and *Untamed Heart* with Marisa Tomei
- 1994, appeared in *It Could Happen to You* with Nicolas Cage
- Choreographer for Bobby Brown, The Boys, Diana Ross, and *In Living Color*
- Currently: single, living in New York

ROSIE PEREZ

When she starred in her first film, she had no prior acting experience— not even in a school play.

She's been called "unconventional." Some have called her "unpretentious." She is often described as a "pint-sized motormouth." But she never went looking to be an actress. In fact, when she starred in her first film, she had no prior acting experience—not even in a school play. Rosie Perez thinks she is probably the least likely candidate to have been discovered by Hollywood. "All through elementary school," Rosie recalls, "I had to take remedial speech classes because I couldn't even say my own name." She called herself Wosie right up until sixth grade.

Rosa Mary Perez was born in 1964 in Greenpoint Hospital in Brooklyn, New York. One of ten children born to Ismael Serrano and Lydia Perez, she spent most of her early childhood in the Bushwick section of Brooklyn. "Growing up with nine brothers and sisters was an early lesson in assertiveness training. In a family like that, you have to compete for attention," Rosie said.

Rosie's father was a merchant marine, and he spent much time at sea, away from the family. But Rosie remembers that her father always doted on her and would write her long letters while he was away. "If I've got an attitude," Rosie says, "it's because my dad souped up my head when I was a little girl."

Her mother had been a singer in Puerto Rico, before she moved to New York. Music always filled the house, and Rosie grew up watching her mother and father dance salsa on weekends and holidays. Rosie developed an interest in dance at a young age. "I always had a secret passion to be a dancer," Rosie said, "so when they had a program for innercity kids, I couldn't wait to go. I was short and stocky—not like the other girls, who were white and willowy. Maybe that's why this lady told me I had no rhythm. I got angry and cursed her out. She told me never to come back." Since Rosie could no longer take dance lessons, she decided to take part in the New York City club scene. Though she was just in her early teens, she would go to the clubs with her older siblings. She put on a lot of makeup to try to make herself look older.

Rosie was always a good student in school. She liked science best of all. When she graduated from high school, she moved to Los Angeles and enrolled at Los Angeles City College and later at West Los Angeles College to study marine biology and biochemistry. She never lost her love of dancing, however. Every evening she would go dancing at local nightclubs. It was there that she got her first glimpse of show business. "Show business is mostly about marketing," Rosie says. "I learned that when I was a college student in L.A. dancing at the clubs. Four different record companies offered me contracts—and I can't sing. All they knew was, she's got the packaging, she's got the look, and that was

▼▼▼▼▼

"I always had a secret passion to be a dancer," Rosie said.

▲▲▲▲▲▲

ROSIE PEREZ

"Four different record companies offered me contracts— and I can't sing."

enough for them. I saw that and I said to my-self, 'Approach this like a business.'" This positive attitude of Rosie's helped her break into lucrative careers, even though she had no past experience.

One night, while Rosie was in college and dancing at a trendy Latin club, the dance coordinator for the television show *Soul Train* saw her and invited her to appear on the show. She received considerable camera time for the few shows she appeared on. While on *Soul Train*, Rosie met Louis Silas, Jr., senior vice president of black music at MCA Records. He asked her if she would like to be in a recording group, but Rosie had no aspirations for the singing business. She declined his invitation but kept in touch with him after she left *Soul Train*.

Eventually, Louis asked Rosie if she would choreograph a video and stage show for singer Bobby Brown, who was relatively unknown at the time. Bobby was coming out with his third solo album, and Louis wanted him to have a younger appeal. He thought Rosie could find some dancers who could dance hip-hop with him. Rosie had no experience whatsoever at choreographing dance routines, and she was inclined to turn down the offer. She told Louis she didn't think she could do it. But then she thought it over for a while. "He told me I could," she said. "He presented the challenge, and I just had to take it." It turns out that Bobby's show was a big hit, and soon she received more offers to choreograph routines for other performing artists. A new Motown recording group called The Boys asked Rosie to choreograph their show. When they, too, became a hit, offers began to pour in. She later choreographed videos or shows for Diana Ross, Heavy D, and LL Cool J.

Then she hit the television screen. Fox TV hired Rosie to be the official choreographer for the Fly Girls on their hit comedy *In Living Color*. Here she brought authentic hip-hop dancing to the American public. The show's creator, Keenen Ivory Wayans, was looking for someone to arrange hip-hop dancing to accompany the show's rap sound track. "I wanted a choreographer who was unconventional, and Rosie is definitely that," he said. Rosie has since been credited with giving the show's dancers a street-smart air that they had previously lacked. Wayans said, "She has taken something raw from the streets and given it a real sense of class and style without losing the essence." Rosie now considers herself a better choreographer than a dancer. She defines her dancing style as "clearness, quickness, and difficult combinations. I haven't seen anyone who can articulate hip-hop the way I do, in such a lean, crisp way, and still be authentic. There are a lot who try to do it, and it comes off very corny. I still got the flavor," she remarks.

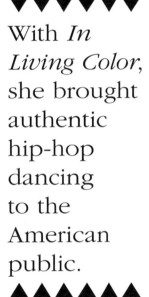

▼▼▼▼▼
With *In Living Color*, she brought authentic hip-hop dancing to the American public.
▲▲▲▲▲▲

ROSIE PEREZ

Rosie's movie career started quite by accident while she was still in college.

Rosie's movie career started quite by accident while she was still in college. She was choreographing the show for The Boys, and she was dancing at the Funky Reggae Club in Los Angeles. One night, while Spike Lee was having his birthday party there, the band EU was playing. "The band asked me to dance on stage," she remembers. "Afterward, Spike Lee introduced himself to me. His partner Monty Ross gave me their phone number and asked me to call. I forgot all about it until about a month later when the school semester was over and I was on my way back to Brooklyn. I decided to call them. They were really excited and asked me if I would be in Los Angeles long. When I told them I was returning to Brooklyn in a couple of days, they started screaming and Spike said, 'This is fate.' I didn't know what he meant by that, because he had never mentioned the possibility of a movie. When I told him I had to return to Los Angeles for the new school semester, he offered me the role of Tina in *Do the Right Thing*. Instead of finishing that semester, I decided to do the movie, and it changed my whole life."

Do the Right Thing (1989) was a very controversial movie about race relations, and it caused a lot of furor when it hit the theaters. It gave an explosive portrait of life on a Brooklyn block on the hottest day of the summer. Originally, Spike had thought of casting a black actress, but he later thought that Rosie was the perfect choice to play Tina, an emotionally demanding young woman who feels neglected by her boyfriend, Mookie, played by Spike Lee. When Robi Reed, Spike's casting director, heard Rosie read for the part, he instantly agreed that she was the ideal choice. "Rosie is a natural," Reed said. "She has no formal acting training, but when she read for me, she was so real that I cried. I called Spike and said, 'She's Tina.'"

Rosie admitted that she had mixed feelings about taking the part. "I was so scared," she said. "But at the same time, I wasn't going to say, 'Well, no, Spike. I'd rather not do this film.'" Rosie describes her first movie part as

Rosie's first movie was with Spike Lee in *Do the Right Thing*.

the best and worst thing that happened to her. She really couldn't relate to her character, Tina, and she later revealed that she wouldn't play another part like Tina again. But this movie was her big break. It launched her acting career.

ROSIE PEREZ

Many actresses attend drama school; some star in local theater productions or take private acting lessons. But Rosie learned her craft by starring on TV and in films. "I'd do a scene with Johnny Depp," she says, "and he'd say, 'Hey, that was pretty good.' So I'd go back in my trailer and scream, 'Johnny Depp said I was good!' But I had no idea how or why I was good, so the whole thing was pretty useless." Rosie found that the less she thought about acting, the more progress she was able to make. She learned more by appearing on CBS's *WIOU* and Fox TV's *21 Jump Street*. In 1990, she starred in the HBO made-for-television movie *Criminal Justice*. Then,

From left to right: Tyra Ferrell (Rhonda), Wesley Snipes (Sidney Deane), Woody Harrelson (Billy Hoyle), and Rosie Perez (Gloria) starred in the Twentieth Century Fox comedy *White Men Can't Jump*.

in 1992, she snared her best part in the highly successful movie *White Men Can't Jump*. It was a giant step for Rosie that put her in the big leagues.

White Men Can't Jump was a movie about two athletic con men (played by Wesley Snipes and Woody Harrelson) who support themselves by hustling basketball games at an outdoor court in Los Angeles. The movie was intended to be a kind of male-bonding movie, but Rosie stole the show with her portrayal of Gloria, the girlfriend of Woody Harrelson's character. Casting Rosie in the part of Gloria was a complete surprise, since Gloria was originally written as an Anglo woman, a college graduate who rebels by running away with a basketball player. But when writer-director Ron Shelton heard Rosie read, he knew she was the right person to play the role. "I couldn't get her out of my head," he said. The fact that she got along well with Woody Harrelson helped to clinch the deal. The script was not changed a great deal to accommodate Rosie. Gloria's character was changed from a Barnard graduate to an ex-disco queen. But, other than that, Rosie played the part as it was originally written.

"I can play a role that was originally for a white woman," Rosie said, "but I could never stop being Puerto Rican. I wouldn't try to act like a white woman. The directions do not say, 'Act

▼▼▼▼▼▼
The movie was intended to be a kind of male-bonding movie, but Rosie stole the show with her portrayal of Gloria.
▲▲▲▲▲▲

ROSIE PEREZ

white.' They say, 'A pretentious woman.' That has no color in it."

The critics loved the movie *White Men Can't Jump.* Many of them cited Rosie as the main reason to go see it. Critic Georgia Brown wrote in the *Village Voice* (April 7, 1992), "The best thing about [Shelton's] engaging comedy is the commanding presence of the shrill, pint-sized motormouth Rosie Perez." Kenneth Turan wrote in the *Los Angeles Times* (March 27, 1992), "It is safe to say that Perez plays it like no one else on the planet . . . To hear Gloria giving Billy a hilarious what-women-want lecture . . . is to feel in the presence of a true screen original."

Marisa Tomei (left) and Rosie Perez played coworkers and best friends in the movie *Untamed Heart.*

Rosie next played supporting roles in two films. *A Night on Earth* was about five taxicab encounters. Rosie played Angela, who becomes embroiled in a screaming match with her brother-in-law, played by Giancarlo Esposito. In *Untamed Heart*, Rosie played Cindy, a feisty waitress whose best friend and coworker Caroline (played by Marisa Tomei) becomes involved with a dishwasher (played by Christian Slater.)

By the time she had finished *Untamed Heart*, Rosie wanted to expand her horizons. She complained that the Latina roles available all portrayed Hispanic women as loud and volatile. She said she now wanted to play a part where she didn't have to scream her lungs out. "I can be Hispanic and play a Jessica Lange role," she said. "All I need is the opportunity to go for it." Her first opportunity came in 1993 when she was cast in *Fearless*, about the survivors of an airplane

Rosie and Jeff Bridges starred in the movie *Fearless*.

ROSIE PEREZ

Rosie played Muriel Lang, whose husband Charlie (played by Nicolas Cage) wins the lottery and decides to give half to a waitress as a tip, in the comedy *It Could Happen to You*. In this photo, Muriel is being charmed by another lottery millionaire (played by Seymour Cassel).

crash. Rosie played Carla, a young Puerto Rican woman who was grieving for the child she lost in the crash. The character was originally written as an Italian-American woman, but once again, the part was rewritten with Rosie in mind. Carla was a guilt-ridden, deeply religious woman, and this role required a much deeper intensity than any Rosie had played before. She rose to the challenge of more serious drama and earned an Academy Award nomination in the best supporting actress category for *Fearless*.

In 1994, Rosie starred in the romantic comedy *It Could Happen to You*. She played Muriel, the loud, screeching wife of the character played by Nicolas Cage. Muriel is outraged when her husband gives half of his four-million-dollar lottery winnings to a waitress as a tip.

In addition to her talent in acting and choreography, Rosie is also a talented businesswoman. In 1993 she was the executive producer for a three-part HBO series called *Rosie Perez Presents Society's Ride*. The show featured live performances by rhythm-and-blues artists, rap singers, and reggae performers. Rosie also manages an all-female rhythm-and-blues band called 5 A.M.

In 1996, Rosie produced *Subway Stories* for HBO, a special based on New Yorkers' true subway tales. She also appeared in the movie, *Somebody to Love*, where her character had to find the strength to end a bad relationship.

Being a Hispanic actress in Hollywood is definitely a challenge. There are few Hispanic actresses to begin with, there are fewer parts for Latinas, and, what's worse, there are even fewer good roles for Latinas. Despite the difficulties that Rosie has faced in this industry, she is determined to succeed. "The racism, the sexism, I never let it be my problem," she said. "It's their problem. If I see a door comin' my way, I'm knockin' it down. And if I can't knock down the door, I'm sliding through the window. I'll never let it stop me from what I want to do."

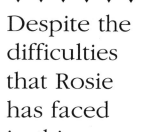
Despite the difficulties that Rosie has faced in this industry, she is determined to succeed.

Cheech Marin

Actor, Director, Writer, Musician
1946-

"The thing I think is most important to emphasize is to work hard, practice, be diligent, do the work, because that's the only way you'll get ahead. Everybody has different degrees of talent or innate attributes, but the only way you develop them is through hard work and diligence and with your nose to the grindstone.**"**

Cheech Marin, as told to Barbara Marvis, May 1996

BIO HIGHLIGHTS

- Born July 13, 1946, Los Angeles; mother: Elsa; father: Oscar Marin
- Moved to Granada Hills at age ten
- 1964, attended California State University at Northridge
- 1968, moved to Canada, where he met Tommy Chong
- 1972, recorded first Cheech and Chong album, *Cheech and Chong*
- 1974, earned Grammy Award for Cheech and Chong's third album, *Los Cochinos*
- 1979, first Cheech and Chong movie, *Up in Smoke*, is released
- 1987, wrote, directed and starred in *Born in East L.A.*
- 1994, released the CD, *My Name is Cheech the School Bus Driver* in English and Spanish
- 1995, starred in *Desperado*
- 1996, starred in *From Dusk Till Dawn, The Great White Hype,* and *Tin Cup.*
- 1996, starred in *Nash Bridges* on CBS
- Currently: married to Patti; he has three children: Carmen from a previous marriage, and Joe and Jasmine with Patti

CHEECH MARIN

In all the roles he's taken in over 25 years in Hollywood, he has always proudly played a Latino.

It's difficult to describe the many faces of Cheech Marin. (Cheech is short for *chicharrón*, a Hispanic delicacy made of deep-fried pork skins.) He has played an easy-living hippie, a *cholo* (homeboy), a misplaced Chicano, and a Mexican revolutionary. But in all the roles he's taken in over 25 years in Hollywood, he has always proudly played a Latino.

Born in 1946 in East Los Angeles, Richard Antonio Marin discovered early on that he had a talent for music; comedy came later. At the age of five, he recorded and released his first song, *"Amorcito Corazon."* He learned to play the guitar when he was twelve, and during his school years he sang with a neighborhood rock band. He earned his nickname, Cheech, as a baby, when his uncle Urbano looked at him in the crib, saw a shriveled baby and remarked, "He looks like a *chicharrón*."

Cheech's parents were born in Los Angeles and are of Mexican descent. He is the third generation of his family to live in the United States. His father, Oscar, was a police officer for the Los Angeles Police Department (LAPD) for over 30 years. After he retired, he taught criminology at Valley College in Los Angeles. Cheech says his father was very authoritarian, and they butted heads a great deal when he was growing up. "Today, though, we get along very well," he reveals.

CHEECH MARIN

Cheech's mother, Elsa, stayed home with the kids. "She was always loving and nurturing," remembers Cheech.

The oldest of four, he and his three sisters, Margie and Monica (twins) and Elena, grew up in an African-American neighborhood in downtown Los Angeles. When Cheech was ten, his family moved to a more mixed neighborhood in Granada Hills. The move from an almost all-African-American neighborhood to an all-white neighborhood in the suburbs made an impression on young Cheech. "I remember the orange groves in Granada Hills," he says. "It was really an idyllic boy's country life."

"Only English was spoken in our house," he said in a 1992 interview to the *Los Angeles Times*. "My parents would speak Spanish with my grandparents when they didn't want me to understand." As an adult, however, he made a point to learn Spanish in order to teach it to his own children.

Cheech was an avid baseball player as a boy, so his early role models were baseball players, including almost any Los Angeles Dodger, such as pitchers Don Drysdale and Sandy Koufax. His most favorite ballplayer, despite the fact that he played for the rival team, the San Francisco Giants, was Willie Mays. "I really loved him. For me, he was the ultimate ballplayer." As far as entertainers or Hollywood figures go, he says,

▼▼▼▼▼

His most favorite ball player was Willie Mays. "I really loved him. For me, he was the ultimate ballplayer."

▲▲▲▲▲▲

CHEECH MARIN

"At the time, there was a dearth of Latino public figures for me to look up to," and, typical of many young boys, baseball was his real obsession.

"My family taught me that education was really important. In our family, education was first and foremost. My dad had a small amount of college, and academics were always stressed—of course, I learned it was important to clean your room, too," he jokes. But learning was always fun for Cheech. "The quest for knowledge became a really exciting factor for me, that and playing sports and the discovery of girls. What else do you need?" Though he says he enjoyed subjects like history and biology, English teachers, such as high-school teacher Father Donovan, encouraged Cheech to study writing and literature.

Educated in Catholic schools, Cheech attended De La Salle Elementary School in San Fernando until eighth grade and then Alemany Catholic High School, where he was a straight-A student. It was in college, he says, that his eyes were opened to the secular world. After working his way through college as a dishwasher and janitor, he quit school only eight credits short of a bachelor of arts degree in English from California State University at Northridge. He opted to take pottery classes and enjoyed them so much—for a short time—he thought he had

▼▼▼▼▼▼
Cheech met Tommy Chong in Vancouver, British Columbia, in Canada.
▲▲▲▲▲▲

found his new calling. But with the escalation of the Vietnam War, this dream was cut short. He chose to move to Canada to avoid the draft. "I had had it with school at that point and was off to seek my fame and fortune. I didn't get the degree, but I got the education, and I thought that was most important. I couldn't unlearn what I had learned."

In the 1960s, Cheech met Tommy Chong in Vancouver, British Columbia, in Canada, and from that association, the improvisational comedy troupe Cheech and Chong was born. By

Cheech (left) with Tommy Chong in *Cheech and Chong's Next Movie*

CHEECH MARIN

Cheech and Chong portray hip ice-cream vendors spreading good humor through the streets of L.A. in *Cheech and Chong's Nice Dreams*

1972, their act, which made fun of the drug culture at the time, took off. They began performing in nightclubs. That year they also approached record maker Lou Adler to make their first comedy album, *Cheech and Chong,* which featured the crazy nun Sister Mary Elephant in charge of a room full of energetic high-school kids. Two years later they had earned four gold albums as well as many top-ten singles, including "Basket Ball Jones." Their third album, *Los Cochinos* (the Dirty Ones), brought them a Grammy Award.

CHEECH MARIN

In 1976, after the release of their album *Sleeping Beauty*, Cheech and Chong stopped making records and started writing scripts for their own movie. Their first effort was *Up In Smoke*, which was released in 1978. The movie's phenomenal success (it cost $2 million to make but earned over $104 million in worldwide box-office ticket sales) established Cheech and Chong as Hollywood darlings.

Chong would direct all six of their next movies, but the movies were a true collaborative effort with equal input from Cheech. He describes his relationship with Chong like this: "It's like music. You know, when you start a riff and the other guy chimes in. We've known each other so long and have such a backlog of experiences together." Before the duo split up in 1985, they released a total of eight movies, including *Cheech and Chong's Next Movie* in 1980, *Cheech and Chong's Nice Dreams* in 1981, *Things Are Tough All Over* in 1983, and *Cheech and Chong's The Corsican Brothers* in 1984.

By the time he decided to make his own movies, Cheech was ready to drop the act of the dope-smoking hippie. Although he made jokes about the uselessness of smoking marijuana in the form of Cheech the character, the real Cheech was not actually the same person he played in his movies. Even reporters who interviewed him at the time seemed surprised at his

▼▼▼▼▼▼
By the time he decided to make his own movies, Cheech was ready to drop the act of the dope-smoking hippie.
▲▲▲▲▲▲

He says he had been trying to break the barrier for Latinos in television for years, but . . . he hadn't been successful.

CHEECH MARIN

"intelligence and articulateness." His partner, Chong, wanted to continue with the same movies, but Cheech was ready to send a new message to Hollywood. He explained his feelings this way in a *Los Angeles Times* interview: "We had grown out of those guys. At some point, it becomes pathetic and not funny." Still, the experience had made him a household name. "I'm real proud of the legacy," he later commented. "It's like having been in the Beatles or the Stones, something that's a part of society and culture. I would never turn my back on that. If it wasn't for that, I wouldn't be here now."

In 1987, Cheech released the first movie in which he not only starred but which he also wrote and directed—*Born in East L.A.* Though some movie critics seemed disappointed (many expected Cheech to bring back his character from his Cheech and Chong days), Latinos did not miss the significant message behind the movie. Looking back, *Born in East L.A.* was surprisingly ahead of its time. It began as a takeoff of the Bruce Springsteen hit "Born in the U.S.A." The movie tells the story of Chicano Rudy Robles, whom the Immigration and Naturalization Service *(la migra)* picks up by mistake and deports to Mexico. Because Rudy's family is out of town and he has no identification with him (he left his wallet at home), he's stuck in Mexico, trying to figure out a way to get back to L.A. As one reviewer described it, "[Cheech] tries so hard to be zany, convincing and eventually serious about the poverty that leads so many Mexicans to cross the border." In a moving moment in the movie, Rudy leads hundreds of Mexicans across the border, overwhelming the Border Patrol, to the tune of Neil Diamond's song "Coming to America." Cheech is very proud of this film. "*Born* was extremely important to me. I had broken up with my partner. I was getting divorced at the same time. I didn't have anything on the horizon except house payments. I knew I

Cheech and Tommy Chong starred with their wives, Rikki Marin and Shelby Fiddis, in *Things Are Tough All Over.*

"'I'm not going to let these guys defeat me. I'm going to make an entry into TV somewhere.'"

wanted to do something else, some kind of social commentary."

Although he did star in one more movie, *Shrimp on the Barbie,* in 1990, and he was the voice of Tito, the streetwise Chihuahua in Disney's animated film *Oliver and Company,* he began to turn his attention to television and music. He says he had been trying to break the barrier for Latinos in television for years, but whether it was his character from the Cheech and Chong movies or simple resistance by television executives, he hadn't been successful. He spent two years developing a series for the Latino comedy troupe Culture Clash for Fox Television, but it never got off the ground. "I had this kind of Latino agenda where I was trying to get this Latino presence on television and get myself rich at the same time," he says. In 1992, he broke through with a role on *Golden Palace,* a spin-off from the *Golden Girls* series about four retired ladies living in Miami, Florida. In the show he played Chuy Castillos, a divorced transplanted Chicano chef with an attitude from Los Angeles. Though the show was canceled, Cheech continued to persevere. "I said, 'I'm not going to let these guys defeat me. I am going to make an entry into TV somewhere, somehow.' I just had to keep lowering my head and banging it through the door. They didn't make my faith in myself falter, but my faith in the whole industry process—I was definitely disillusioned."

In 1994, Cheech was cast in the TNT movie *Cisco Kid* in the role of Pancho. The film starred Jimmy Smits as Cisco and was directed by Luis Valdez. The story, based on O. Henry's "The Caballero's Way" takes place during the Mexican Revolution in the late 1800s, which culminated in the famous battle won by a small Mexican army, on May 5, against the French in 1862. This victory is still celebrated today in Mexico but even more enthusiastically in the U.S. as *el Cinco de Mayo*. Cisco is a man in search of his identity. He was born in California, when it was still part of Mexico, but fought in the Civil War as an American. He travels to Mexico on a secret mission from the U.S. government to supply guns to Mexican rebels, and that's where he meets Pancho, a Mexican revolutionary. "Cisco is probably the first Chicano," commented Smits, a New Yorker of Puerto Rican descent. "There is a whole question of identity: 'Where do I belong?'" The role of Pancho was particularly attractive to Cheech because it's Pancho, the man committed to his country—Mexico—and to the revolution, that helps Cisco find his identity.

Cheech Marin has plugged away at his career in Hollywood for over 25 years.

As a parent, he wanted to create something his kids could relate to, and he wanted to satisfy his own desire to return to music.

CHEECH MARIN

About this same time, Cheech also began a new project. Never leaving his first love, music, and being the father of three, he began to work on a CD for children, *My Name Is Cheech the School Bus Driver*, which was also released in Spanish as *Me Llamo Cheech, el Chofer del Autobus de la Esquela*. Lou Adler, who had produced the Cheech and Chong records, approached Cheech about recording the CD. Adler had produced several children's records at the time, but it was his wife who noticed that few records existed for bilingual children. The project appealed to Cheech for two reasons. As a parent, he wanted to create something his kids could relate to, and he wanted to satisfy his own desire to return to music. The songs are fun to listen to. Targeted at elementary-school children, Cheech prepares the children on the bus for a full day of school, beginning with art class and the song, "Red and Blue and Yellow Too." He also teaches bigger lessons with songs like "Trading Lunches," which not only encourages kids to explore new worlds through food but also to learn about their classmates. Cheech sings: "You could trade a bowl of guacamole for a plate of ravioli or a cup of minestrone for a ham and cheese on rye. Maybe a cup of Chinese noodles for a hunk of apple streudel or maybe something you never ever tried." The lesson is reinforced with the refrain: "Trading lunches, you might eat something from Greece. Trading lunches could bring about world peace."

He also teaches a little English or Spanish, depending on the version of the CD, with the song, "Tell Me How Do You Say," *"Dime Como Se Dice."* Songs like this one were really important to him, he says. "I strongly support bilingual education, and it worries me that as each generation distances itself further from Mexico, we lose the language of our heritage." His album became a great success, and the Los Angeles School District even used one of his songs to teach kids about how to mix and use colors. In 1996 he released a second album: *My Name*

Cheech portrayed a bartender in the lawless border town of Santa Cecilia in *Desperado.*

CHEECH MARIN

is Cheech the School Bus Driver "Coast to Coast." According to Cheech, "The music speaks directly to kids in an intelligent way—the songs are fun, but educational."

The CDs also gave him a chance to use the Tex-Mex sound in his songs. "Tex-Mex music is complicated and simple at the same time," he explains. "I believe, in the future, these rhythms will be our children's popular music."

By 1995, Cheech's movie career took another positive turn. He starred in Robert Rodriguez's movie *Desperado,* a sequel to Rodriguez's first movie, *El Mariachi.* Immediately after that, he also appeared in Rodriguez's next movie, *From Dusk Till Dawn*, where he played three characters, most notably a border patrol officer, for which he actually shaved his signature mustache. Working with the 27-year-old director was memorable for Cheech as well as for Rodriguez. In a 1995 *L.A. Life* interview, Marin describes Rodriguez as "the real deal." He continues, "There's a creative flow that goes through him that is unadulterated. And he's the quickest guy I've ever worked with, bar none."

According to Rodriguez, he had been trying to fill the role for *From Dusk Till Dawn* without much success. In the same interview he says, "I had a number of actors read it and it didn't

Cheech played several roles in *From Dusk Till Dawn.* He played a border guard, Chet Pussy, and the mysterious Carlos.

play at all. Then Cheech read it, and I thought, 'Oh my God, this is gonna be gold.'" Also in 1995, Cheech was the voice of Banzai, one of the dastardly hyenas in Disney's *The Lion King.*

He starred in two more movies in 1996. Along with Samuel Jackson, Jeff Goldbloom, and Damon Wayans, he starred in *The Great White Hype,* in which he played a character modeled after the Latino head of the World Boxing Council.

Cheech plays Joe Dominguez on *Nash Bridges*

"The character's just a toady, basically," he says. He also starred in *Tin Cup* along with Kevin Costner as a golf caddy and Costner's best buddy. He reentered the television arena in the CBS television drama *Nash Bridges* with Don Johnson. *Nash Bridges* is set in San Francisco, and Cheech plays Johnson's longtime friend and partner Joe Dominguez. "It's a cop show," he says, "but a lot of it takes place off duty. It explores their personal and familial relationships, and it has a lot of humor. Don Johnson is a wonderful guy to work with, and I love filming in San Francisco. The show has been picked up again for the fall of 1996." After years of knocking on the door to the world of television, Marin seems genuinely pleased with this show. Persistence and hard work eventually do pay off.

Hollywood, especially for Latinos, has its ups and downs. Cheech hopes to keep working as much as he can.

CHEECH MARIN

From his experiences, Cheech has this advice for young people today: "The thing I think is most important to emphasize is work hard, practice, be diligent, do the work, because that's the only way you'll get ahead. Everybody has different degrees of talent or innate attributes, but the only way you develop them is through hard work and diligence and with your nose to the grindstone."

Cheech has three children: his daughter from a previous marriage, Carmen, 17; and Joe, 11, and Jasmine, 4, with his wife Patti. Hollywood, especially for Latinos, has its ups and downs. Cheech hopes to keep working as much as he can, but he also wants to spend more time with his family and doing the things he loves to do, like writing and collecting Chicano art. He owns one of the largest collections of Chicano art, over 100 pieces. "I've always been interested in art, since grade school. I educated myself about art from the time I was in fifth or sixth grade." Once he got older and could afford to buy it, he began collecting. "Not only did I want to encourage these artists, their work was the best, regardless of race, and the art spoke to me more clearly than any other art I'd seen." Just as these artists spoke to him, Cheech's work, his talent, and his sincerity will continue to speak to Latinos and to all audiences, on TV, on CD, and in movies.

Index